Aa
B
Dd
Ee
Ff
Gg
Hh
Ii
Jj
Kk
Ll
Mm
Nn
Oo
Pp
Qq
Rr
Ss
Tt
Uu
Vv
Ww
Xx
Yy
Zz

Zip

Zip is a friendly space alien from planet Zee. He loves to learn. Zip uses his hands to speak to his friends. He can't wait to teach the people of planet Earth all about sign language. Zip is the captain of his spaceship.

Pella

Pella is Zip's best friend. She also comes from planet Zee. Pella is very brave. Although she is a little younger than Zip and Statz, she isn't afraid of anything and is always the first of the three friends to try new things.

Statz

Statz is in charge of computers on the spaceship. He loves gadgets. Statz uses his Zablet to help him and his friends out of sticky situations. He is excited to learn about planet Earth and all the people who live here.

Goober

Goober is an unexpected guest on the friends' adventures. A greedy and naughty space stowaway, Goober has the ability to change his colour and shape so is always jumping out and surprising Zip, Pella and Statz.

Zip's top tips

Zip and friends are here to help you talk in a fun new way - spell with your fingers and talk with your hands. Follow these top tips to get the most from their adventures:

- **Share the book together and enjoy the story**
- **Play with the signs**
- **Use Zip's alphabet to make your own words**
- **Visit Space School, enjoy the activities and have fun**
- **Watch out for Goober...**

SignSpell

Zip and the Party

Party

The spaceship has landed in a pretty garden next to a little house.

Zip, Pella and Statz can see that something is going on inside. There is music playing and lots and lots of brightly coloured balloons.

"What's going on here?" asks Pella.

Statz checks his Zablet. "Someone is having a party," he tells his friends. They can't wait to go inside.

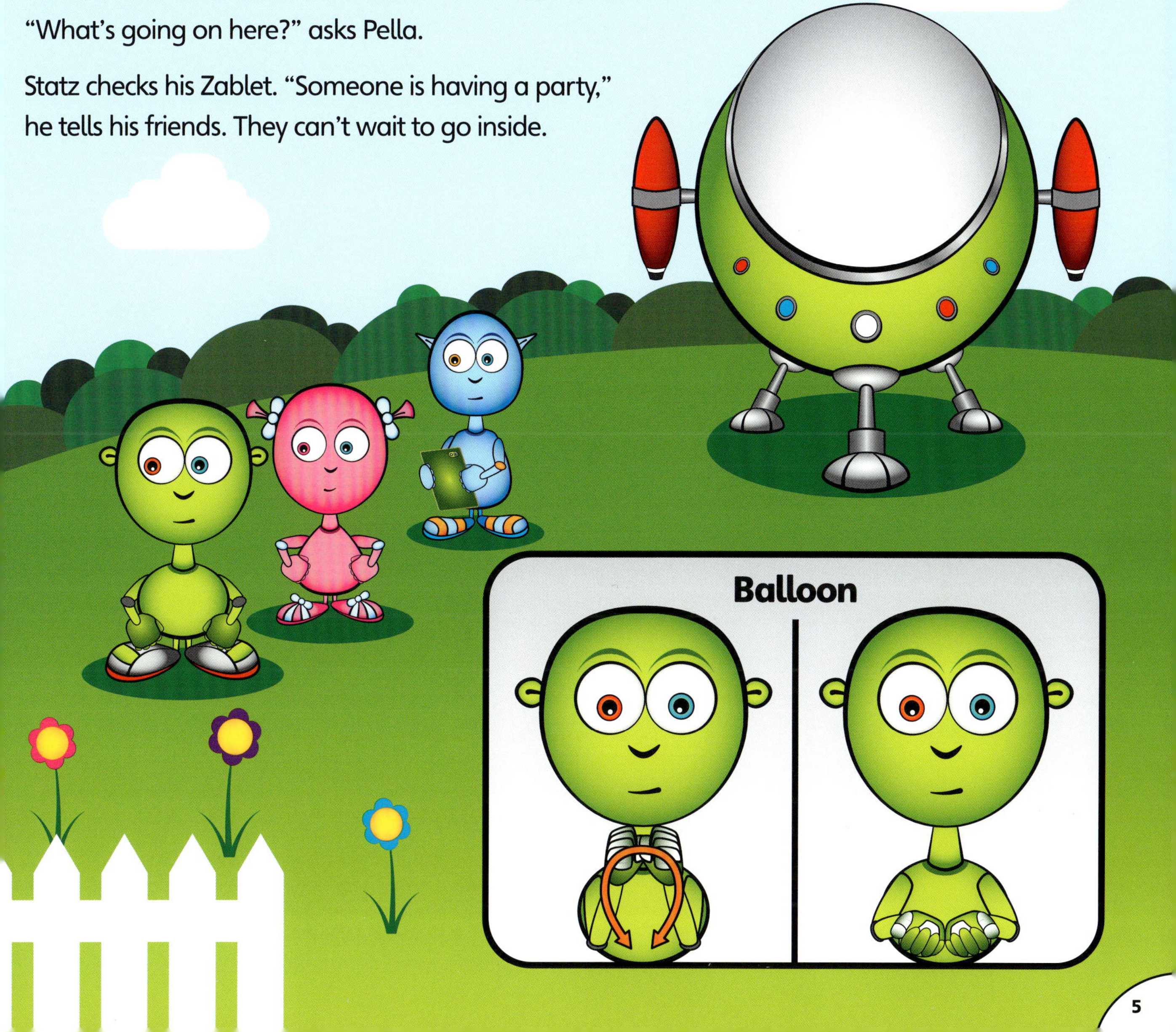

Zip thinks about the last party he had on planet Zee. He invited all his friends and he gave each of them a present to celebrate his birthday.

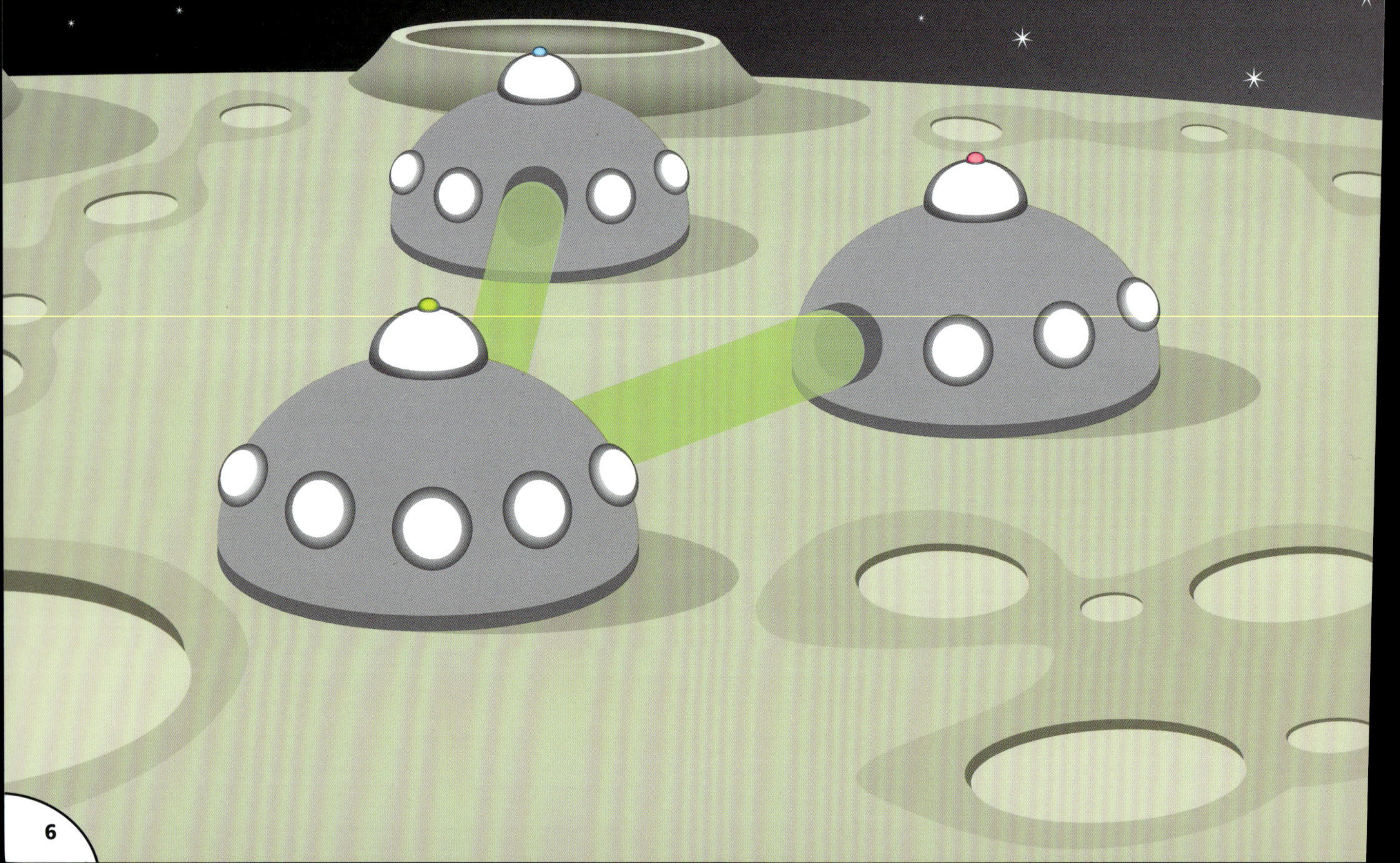

His pod was decorated with floating sparkles and his friends ate as many frozen sherbet rocks as they could.

Game
GAMES
GAMES
BOARD GAMES

The friends go into the house and find games piled on the floor.
"We could have some real fun here," says Zip.
"It's a shame we don't know how to play any of them."

"Don't worry," says Statz,
"I'll look up the rules on my Zablet."

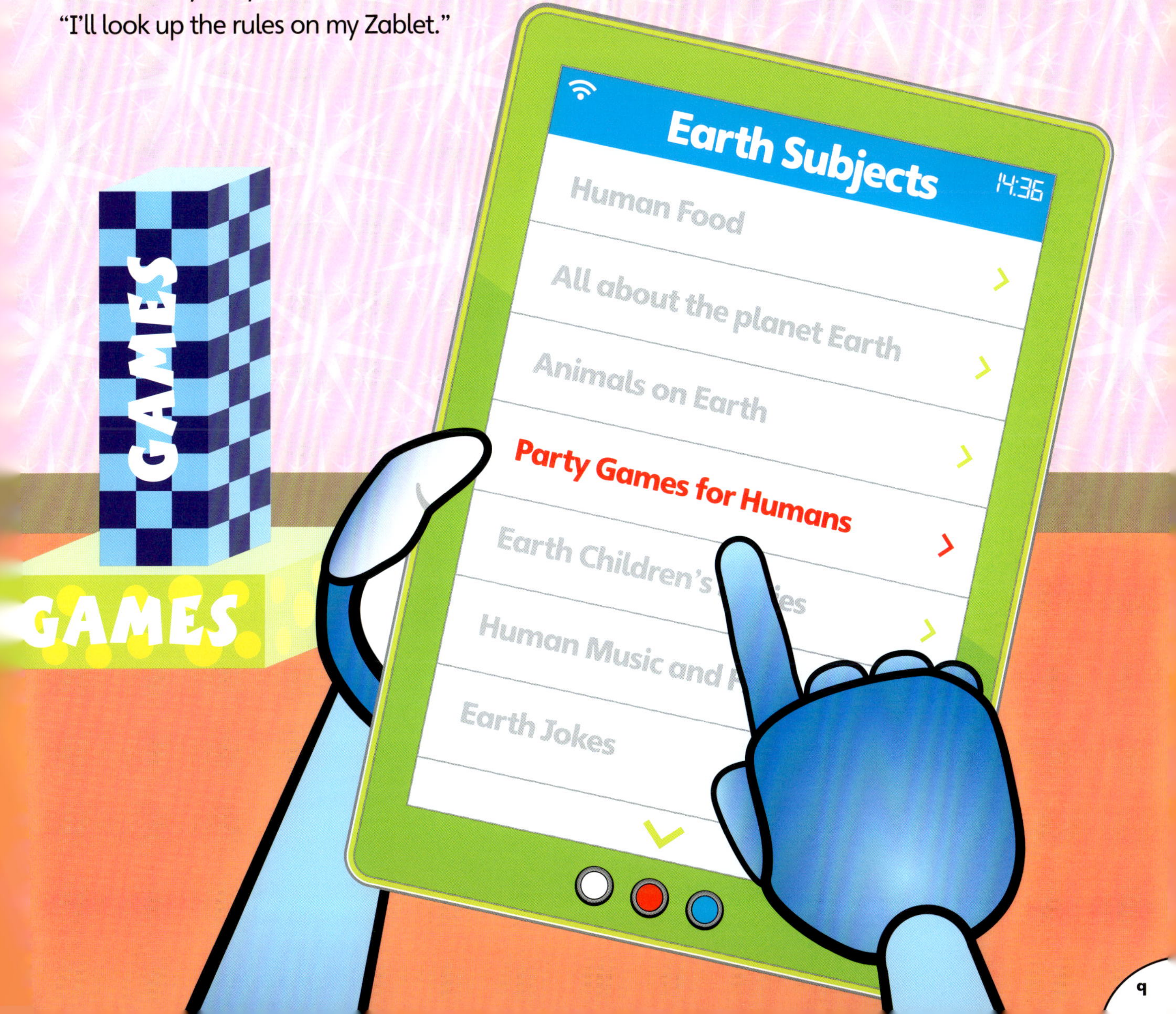

Zip runs over to a big picture of a donkey that is pinned to the wall.
"Is this a game?" he asks. "How do we play?"

"This is a game called Pin the Tail on the Donkey," says Statz.
"Humans put a blindfold on and try to pin a tail on the donkey's bottom."

Pella thinks this is very funny.

"That sounds easy!" says Zip.

Statz explains the rules for the game. “One person plays at a time,” he says. “The player wears a blindfold and is spun round three times before they play.”

“This doesn’t sound so easy now,” says Zip.

Pella puts the blindfold on Zip and spins him around. He steps forward and pins the tail exactly where he thinks it should go.

“Ouch!” says Statz. “I’m not the donkey!”

Better luck next time Zip!

Earth Subjects
Party Games For Humans

Zip has another go. This time his attempt is very good.

"Well done, Zip," says Statz. "You get to choose a prize."

Zip chooses a very, very big green lollipop.
"It looks just like planet Zee!" says Statz.

Space School

Take a look at the pictures below; you may have seen them in the story.
See if you can spell each one using Zip's alphabet.

After all the excitement Zip, Pella and Statz are ready to eat.

In the next room there is a big table covered with lovely party food. There are sandwiches and hot dogs, jelly and ice cream and cheese and pickled onions on sticks.

Zip can't wait to try the jelly. "I've never seen anything so wobbly!" he says.

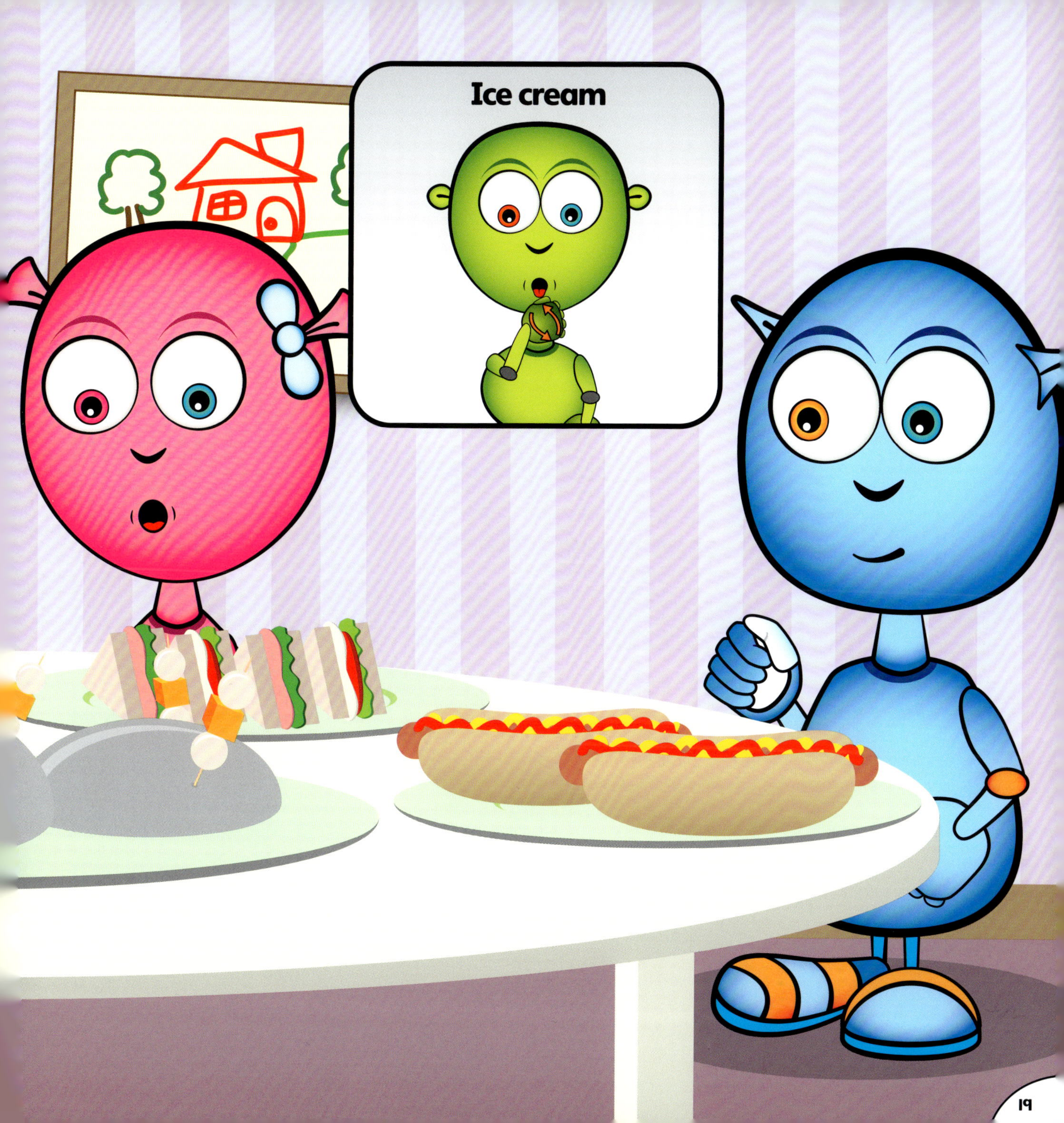
Ice cream

"Oh no!" shouts Pella, "there's a spikeygog trying to eat the food!"

Spikeygogs are from planet Zee. They are very greedy animals that eat anything they can find. A table full of party food would disappear very quickly if a spikeygog got into the room.

"That's not a spikeygog, Pella," laughs Statz.
"It's cheese and pickled onions on sticks!"

Food

Zip, Pella and Statz try all the different types of party food. They each pile a plate full of tasty treats and eat it all.

They are all so full they can rest their plates on their tummies!

"I'm tired after eating all that food," says Zip, "I think it's time for a nap."

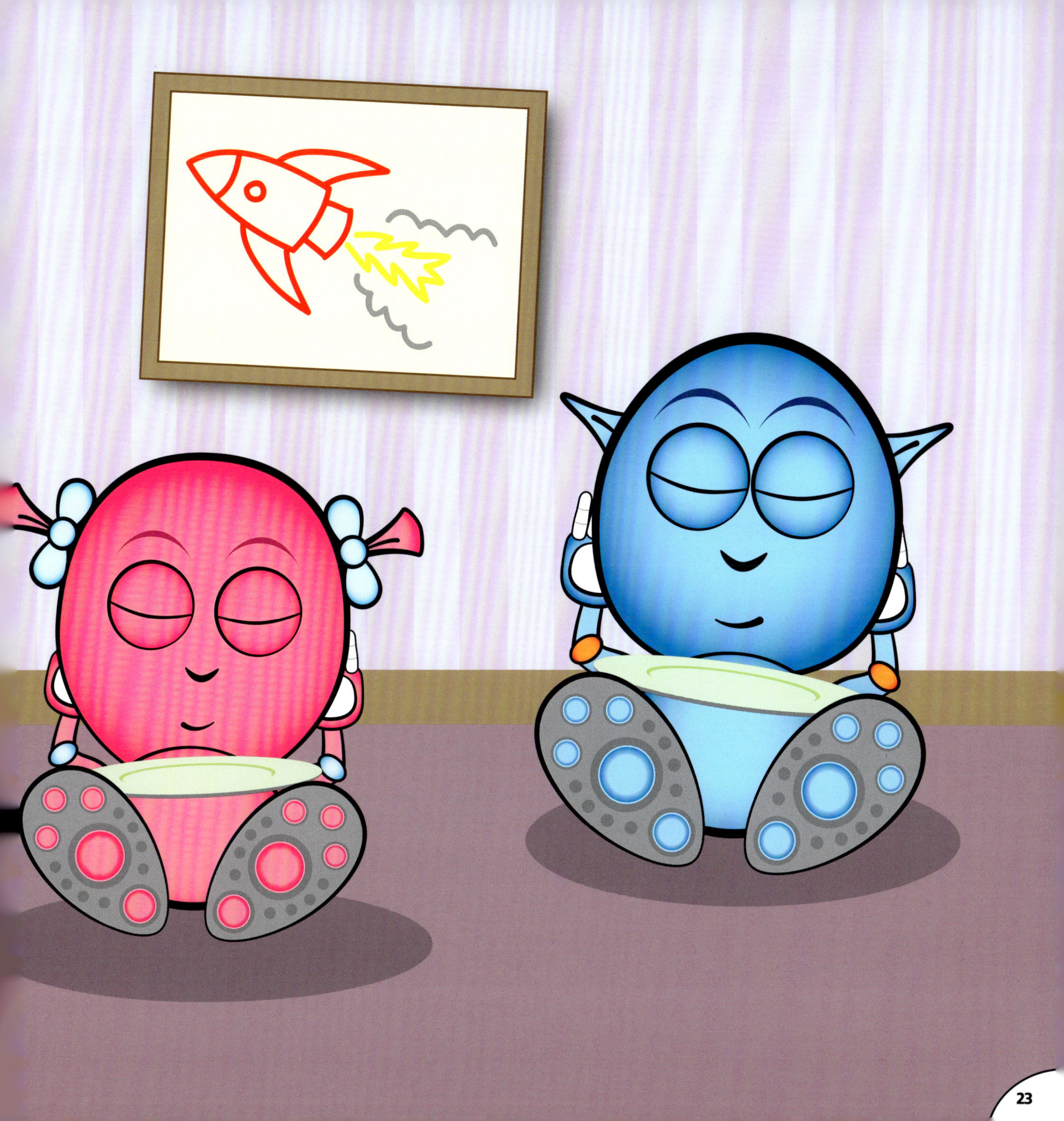

Space School

Take a look at the party invitation below.
Can you see some of the words you have learnt to sign from the story?
See if you can remember how to sign them.

Party invitation

You are invited to my party.

Come along, eat lots of food
and play lots of games.

Party
Balloon
Ice cream
Candle
Games
Jelly
Cake
Food

The friends wake up and get ready to go back to the spaceship. On their way through the house they find a huge birthday cake topped with a pretty pink candle.

“Wow!” says Pella, “I have never seen such a big cake.”

Statz can’t believe what he is seeing. “I want some right now,” he says.

Cake

Suddenly the whole cake disappears before their eyes. There are only a few crumbs left on the plate.

"Where has it gone?" asks Zip.

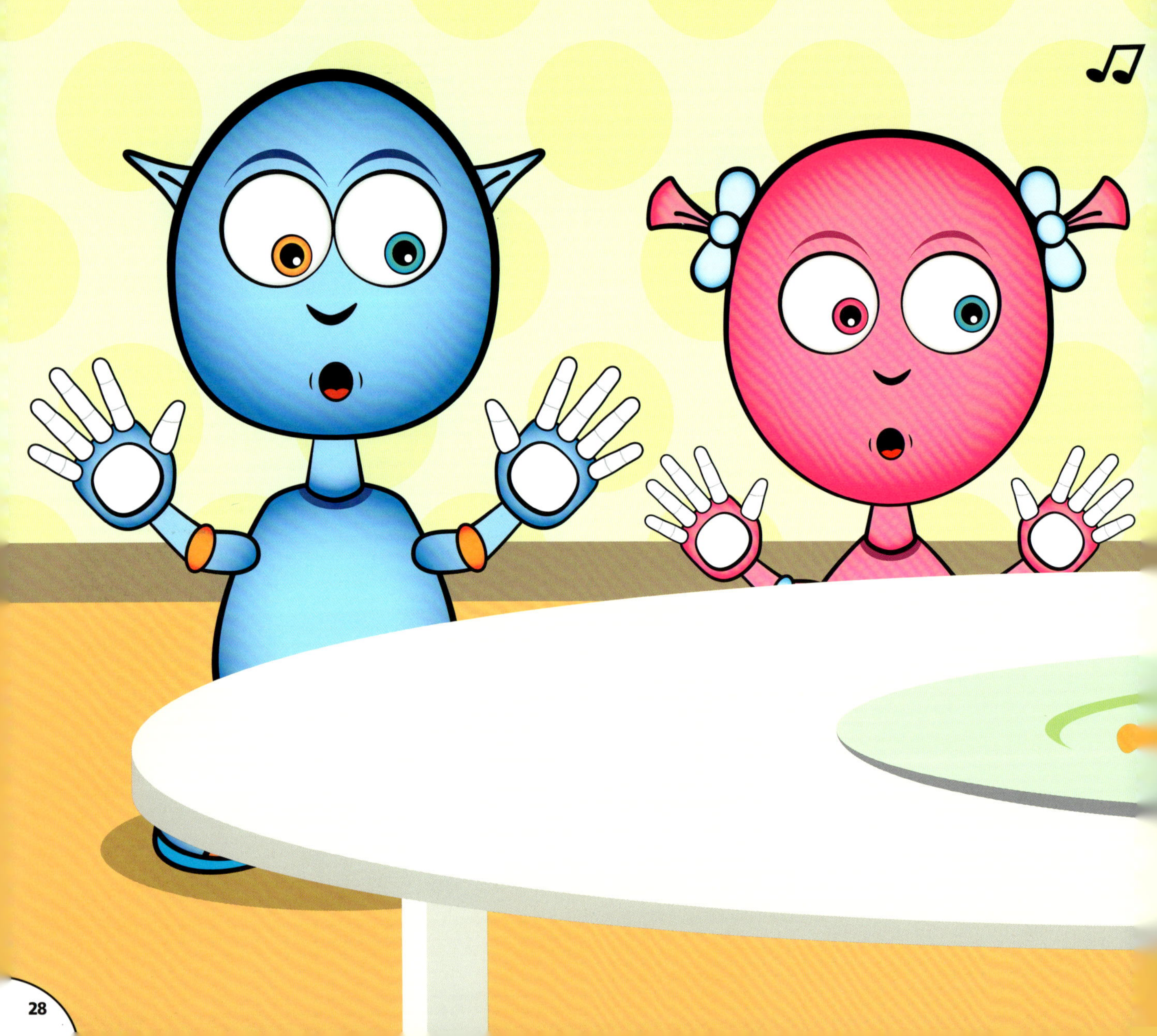

GOOBER!

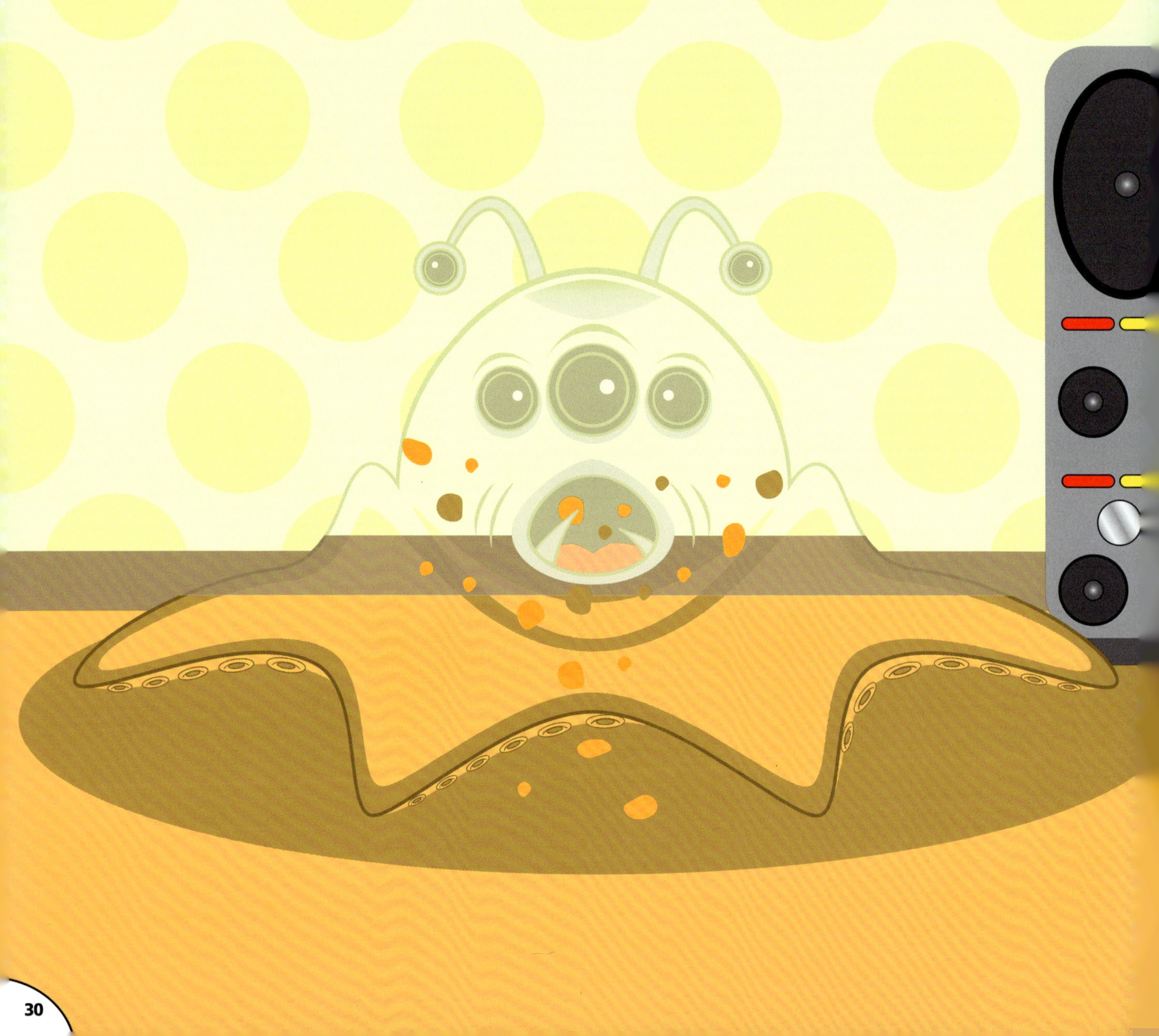

Zip's Signs

Party
Balloon
Present
Birthday
Games
Jelly
Ice cream
Food
Candle
x2
Cake

Fun things to do

Now that you have read all about Zip and the Party,
here are some fun things for you to do:

- **Create your own party - draw, make or act**
- **On planet Zee, what food would they eat at a birthday party?**
- **Draw the best cake ever**
- **How would you feel if someone ate all your cake?**
- **What would you do if there was a spikeygog on your school dinner table?**
- **Teach a friend the sign for jelly and how to spell it**

First published 2013 by Signature

SignSpell® stories created by Signature
Designed and illustrated by Igloo Imaging Ltd.